Driving One Hundred

Driving One Hundred

Poems

Barbara Drake

Windfall Press   Portland, Oregon

First Edition

Windfall Press
P.O. Box 19007
Portland, OR 97280-0007
http://www.hevanet.com/windfall/

Barbara Drake. 1939—
Driving One Hundred

ISBN: 978-0-9700302-1-4

Library of Congress Control Number: 2009934553

Cover photo by Barbara Drake
Cover and book design by Cheryl McLean
Back cover author photo by William Beckman

Printed in the U.S.A.

To my family: here's to the laden table, the bonfire on the beach, the trails through the woods, and all of life's celebrations.

CONTENTS

PART 3

Part One

DRIVING ONE HUNDRED

We went, in 1956, in Sarah's boyfriend's car
out on the new highway south of Coos Bay,
toward Millington, named for a mill,
and the Shinglehouse Slough,
where years later someone's father's ashes
would be scattered, his last wish.
We went in Sarah's boyfriend's car,
a black convertible,
and she, wishing to try on speed,
drove fast, fast, faster,
pushing the speedometer to sixty,
seventy, eighty, as we screamed
and laughed and held ourselves down
in the seats without seatbelts.
Our hair in the wind lashed us
like something breaking over a waterfall,
and afraid our young meat and bones
would be scattered,
we screamed at Sarah, slow down slow down,
Sarah, and then she did ninety
laughing, "He'll kill me if he ever finds out,
you guys, don't tell," and pushed the pedal
down and held it, as we went fast, and faster,
screaming and dying and laughing at Sarah,
until the needle stood at one hundred,
and Sarah relented, and we chided her then,
and began to breathe again,
at sixty, fifty, forty, did a U at twenty,
turned around at the cutoff to Coquille.
 "I almost died," we all said.
"I'll never do that again."
And our flesh settled down to go on living
as we secretly thanked her, like a goddess,
for the terrible experience.

HARD HITTER

Playing softball in grade school
I was a hard hitter once,
just for a week though.
In Crescent City, California,
we lived in a motel by the beach.
Dad thought we'd move there.

The first time we went out to play at recess
I hit the ball way out in the field,
and every time after that, when I came up to bat
the others would yell, "Move back, she's
a hard hitter!" And I was.

I hit ball after ball, like never before.
And never again, after we left
in the middle of the night
and went somewhere else.
I was a different person that week,
hitting the ball with a crack
and everyone moving back,
calling out, "Hard hitter!

WHEN THE AIRPLANE STOPPED

When father's airplane stopped
and we were mid-air,
the little yellow cub continued riding
along on chilly emptiness
like a boat in a stream.
Not a heavy thing at all,
it seemed a toy plane
of paper and balsa wood
tossed up with no rider
but the painted outline
of a soldier, his helmet
and goggles classic, his head
bent to the controls.

Father coughed and grinned
to a grimace, and I said, "Anything wrong?"
"Damn thing went off," he answered.

The bay looked long and blue and beautiful
against the sand spit;
the air was also blue, and chilly.
"Ice," said father,
"in the carburetor."
And still we floated
in that nothingness,

with nothing to fear,
the nothing under us.

And father fiddled with the starter
as the ailerons rowed space
and then before we'd really lost
much altitude, maybe none, maybe
we even gained some,
the engine started and father smiled
and said, "I could land
this plane anywhere, engine or not:
a jetty, a dune, a country
highway. I could have taken it down."

The little plane coasted
along on its putputput of an engine
till we landed where mother sat
in the car at the railing,
and, "What were you doing up there?"
she asked us. "It looked funny."
We said,
"Flying."

THE SMELL OF MAN

Father said, a man in Hawaii,
a retired cop on vacation,
told him:
if you want to find a man in the woods
you dig out a little hole with your hands
in the dirt
and sniff in the hole.
Put your nose to the ground and sniff,
then stand up on your hind legs
and sniff again.
If there's a man around, you'll smell him.

What makes a man's smell so different from dirt?
Different enough. His smell
would stand out in a woods like garlic,
like a thief in church,
like a red silk scarf in a desert.
Imagine the man's smell, an intimate orange spot
against the green odor of fir boughs.
You would meet it, startled,
like sitting on a toilet to pee
and the seat's warm
from someone you don't know
who's been sitting there.

The retired cop said *a man*.
Maybe a woman
would smell more like dirt, like a woods.
He definitely said, "If you want to find a man."
But what is the man's smell?

Is he frightened?
Is the man sweating?
Does he smell of piss or blood

or the oil from his scalp or tobacco?
What is it that makes him
so different from dirt
that no matter what tree he hides in,
whatever ravine he lies down in
like an old log,
no matter how still, how he stops
his breathing or his mouth dries up,
you can still smell him?
Close your eyes.
The hole in the ground, the dirt and the mould,
the fiddlehead ferns unfolding
are not the man.
The wet stones of the creek bed
admit no smell of him.
The fishy flat belly of the salamander,
the rank dry odor of mouse,
the passing odor of violets
are not the man,
nor is the tangy chalk of bird droppings,
the ripe smell of mushrooms.
The citrus attraction of sour grass.
The honeyed blessing of clover.
These are the odors
of earth without man.
But now, you smell it,
like an oily thumb print on glass
or the salt in your own spittle.
You've found him.

PERSEIDS

August 1945

One night it was said
there would be falling stars all night.
I was six and allowed to stay up late
to see them. My friend Billy and I
stood in the street in front of our house—
the street was safe back then—
and watched stars fall.

One after another, they streaked
across the dark sky.
We counted them until
it seemed there were few stars left.
We wondered which would be next.
We wondered where they fell.

When our mothers gathered us in
we looked back over our shoulders,
amazed yet fearing
that the sky would never
again be as bright
as before the stars fell out of it,
like spilled salt, like sand,
like scratches on film or
bubbles in a water glass
left all night on the bed stand.

Now the sky
was so much darker
than it had been.

A MAN I ONCE KNEW

He was a college teacher. Raised a Catholic boy
by Jesuits, he liked to dress up in women's clothes.
His first wife, a South American, said she was innocent.
For all she knew, all American men were like that.
They had three children. Later he had an affair,
divorced his wife, and married
the younger woman. Then they also had three children,
two fat little girls and a baby boy.
His first three children started acting up
and the ex-wife married a librarian.

One time my friend came to our house to visit
while his second wife was out of town
visiting her relatives in Minneapolis.
He called and said, "I'm all dressed up
and nobody to parade for," so we said
he could parade for us. We picked him up
in our old ambulance, the car we were driving
at that time.

He was wearing his hostess skirt
and a long dark wig, a sweater with rhinestones
and a low neck, lots of jewelry, ankle strap
shoes. We had tacos for dinner and he
paraded around a bit,
then ate some tacos.
My kids said they'd never seen anything like it.

Later, he took his family south on a Fulbright,
one of many such honors he'd had. In Rio he had a facelift,

to get rid of the wrinkles and dewlaps. He told me,
"I used to look good, but I got too fat,"
when he dressed up once and invited me over for a drink.
His makeup was thick and white
and his whiskers were black and bristly,
and until he grew his hair out
and had the transplant, he wore untidy wigs at home,
and long velvet skirts and low neck blouses,
lots of heavy bracelets.

In Brazil, he not only got a facelift but also
a hair transplant and had electrolysis on his beard.
He said they cut the hair plugs
out of the back of his head and moved them up front.
He had to go around for several days
with dried blood on his head and face
till the plugs took. They used curare,
he said, to do the job,
and all the time he was paralyzed by the drug,
he could hear and see, but they treated him
as if he were a dead man.

When he and his wife came back with the kids
from Brazil, the plastic surgeon,
who was a beautiful woman, came with them.
She was fed up with being a plastic surgeon
in Brazil, tired of moving hair, carving faces.
She and his wife became lovers
and started a business making hand sewn ethnic
clothes which they tried to sell from a boutique

across from the university.
The ethnic clothes business wasn't so great.

He wanted the surgeon to be
a doctor again, so they'd have more money.
She studied to get her license in the United States
and ended up working in the morgue at a local hospital,
a plastic surgeon fixing up dead people.
She got fed up with that too.
Then his wife got mad and decided to leave him.
She said he was crazy and tried to run over him
with the car so he wouldn't get custody of the children.
He said she tried to kill him
but only broke his arm.
Now he and the plastic surgeon live in the house alone.
He's had several books published
and is a full professor with tenure and a nice salary.

What I want to say is,
clothes don't matter to me that much.

MY FIRST APARTMENT

My first apartment was on southwest eleventh
just up a block from Karafotias Greek grocery
and down a block from Montgomery Gardens.
The first night I spent there, I accidentally
locked myself out and had to go upstairs
and knock on the door of the guy who lived there.
Introduced myself, of course. He did too.
A college student, he worked part-time selling ladies' shoes.
"Locked myself out," I said. "Can I climb out your window
and down the fire escape?"

Unfortunately, I found my window was locked
so I was stuck, but he let me stay
and all night long we listened to music,
talked, drank beer, fooled around a little—nothing much.
Fell asleep on the couch.

About three a.m.
a couple down the hall started fighting.
"You did this..." "You did that..."
"I never did...." "You damned liar...."
It went on and on, until finally
the guy pushed the woman out in the hall.
She was stark naked.
Then the cops came
and things quieted down.

In the morning, my roommate arrived, moving in.
She had a key. I told her about spending the night
with a shoe salesman, listening to people fighting,
seeing that woman, and then the police coming.
I never locked myself out again.
Still, I thought it was a good start,
my first night in my first apartment.

IN THE DARK ROOM

My teeth feel feverish, I ache
from driving yesterday.
Outside the window a goose sighs.
The dog looks at me, wondering
if she can have a piece of my toast.
My toast is slightly black today, carbon
makes a good filter. Charcoal toast
sweetens the stomach, whitens the hot teeth.

She is still watching. Her dear, hairy
little chin trembles.
Noblesse oblige,
time now, to hand over the dog's due,
one bite with grape jelly.
Lace of curtains woven by my husband
softens hints of the day's reality.
Now the geese go, all in a line
down the driveway. If they challenge cars
I'll hear a horn honking.
One by one down the side of a road
was called Indian fashion by Sandra's mother.
It was 1945, summer of my first communion.
Imagine it, one by one the years.

Finally in my father's darkroom
surrounded by clocks and extension cords
I opened the film cans he labeled
in the summer of 1992 before he died.
"Can you find the ones of the farm?" I asked him then.
"Of course, of course, they're all here."
I wasn't sure. Thought he'd lost the old ones.
But last week I found everything:

1944, 1945, bright colors of old transparencies—
luminescence of gelid silver on film, on paper,
shines through the years.
Hello baby sister, hello old dog, hello 1957,
hello sailboat, hello my high school graduation.
A field, a farm, a war year river
flowing away from us down to the sea,
incontrovertible proof of what was.

My father liked my geese though they'd bite
his pants leg. He'd tease them with his fingers,
pinching beaks and taunting the ganders,
come in the house saying, "Look at that,"
showing the bite that broke the skin,
as if he were surprised.
But the old gander
would mostly bow and posture
a greeting expressed in the most courteous of goose gestures
as father took his picture.

All this film, rolled, labeled, and put away
so neatly: *family; little theater; Polish ship; kids;
Kansas; Crystal Creek; Hawaii; Eastern Oregon...*
A lifetime of seeing.
I'm getting old. This child
with her braids pulled back, this child
sitting on the porch railing,
who was she? I think I have been
more than one person.
We have all been more than one person,
stutter of selves like movie footage.

Driving back home, I looked for elk at Reedsport.
It was almost dark but suddenly there they were,
moving, dense hairy giants patterned by light and dark.
The sign said: *pull off here to watch*
them safely from your car.

I pulled off, looked my eyes full, then drove on.
The river seemed higher than the road,
higher than my eyes even.
I stared straight out
and saw how full it was.
Across the water, an old river house was breaking up.
I thought—*Next flood time it'll wash away completely.*

IN THE EYE OF ONE
WHO LOVES YOU

The dunes fill the picture,
their ribbed surfaces like sand at low tide,
the shadows behind each dune
black as the far side of the moon.
And there is my mother, a tiny figure
walking across the sand.

I imagine she likes looking at this photograph
because it reminds her of being
in my father's eye as, from a distance
he took the picture. He is gone now,
but in this picture he always has
his eye on her.

BLACKBOARD

If all of the words that have ever been written on this blackboard,
all the words that ever sank into its flatness and disappeared,
were to rise and come back like the ghosts of ancient professors
they would mutter such a Babel of suggestion—
ontological phenomena the hypotenuse of the disparate
cradle of civilization psychological realism George Eliot
otherwise known as gross national product mechanistic theory
of Darwinian abstract expressionism carrying capacity—
that maybe, just maybe, we could read them one by one
and know what we never knew and remember all we have forgotten.

WATCHING

She used to throw us out of her house
on a regular basis.
I can understand it, actually,
the difficult son, the snotty
educated daughter-in-law,
the impertinent beautiful children—
it was years ago.

I don't want to die alone
but I've felt that way,
wanting space around myself,
space empty as the white light in a refrigerator.
I get fed up with other people sitting there
watching television.

When she died,
she was alone watching television.
Nobody found her at first.
She continued to watch it
for a day or so.

I imagine her lying there,
all day, all night,
through the soaps, the news, the Tonight Show,
all those ads, the late late movies,

a space of darkness,
and then, like resurrection,
the morning cartoons.

During any television show
there are probably a lot of dead people watching
until somebody finds them
and turns it off.

I used to watch a lot of television myself
when we stayed at her house,
before she threw us out, as she did each time.
I watched out of boredom, I suppose, sitting there
waiting to go back to my own house, visiting her
with the kids and my ex-husband.
I'd read the magazines she had,
like *Reader's Digest* or
Ladies Home Journal.
Once in a while I'd copy out a recipe
I'd never get around to making.

Honestly, I don't blame her at all
for chasing us out the door when her temper snapped.
My kids were talking back.
Her son owed her gratitude or money, I forget which.
She considered me a show-off—

I'd once served her espresso coffee and she hated it,
"That dirty foreign crap," an insult.

How well I remember the couch she lay on,
the blue plush pattern, the doilies that fell
down into the cushions when the kids
climbed onto the back, the coffee table
with the magazines, on the wall a rack
of ornamental coffee spoons painted with flags
from various countries she'd never been to,
knick-knack shelves of pixies and salt shakers,
the ivy-patterned wallpaper.

I remember the flickering blue and white
as the sky outside went dark.
There were nylon curtains and a drape
of orange and gold flowered cloth
at the window by the couch.
Out this window one looked
at a chain link fence,
a little white dog on a rope,
and the street.
When I turn it on in my brain,
it all plays back again
like a television.

THE MOTHER

Now that the children are older
there are times she forgets
the attentiveness
of the younger mother.
An evening goes by
in the quiet house.
She forgets to ask:
are they in,
are they out?

Maybe two are out
and the other one in,
but quietly doing something
that doesn't attract her attention.
Then all of a sudden she stops
and wonders and counts—
in or out?
And the ones that are out
she counts coming back,
that one in, one still out,
and so on,
until all are in.
One of these days
they'll go live somewhere else.

She imagines herself
suddenly looking around
for something she ought
but can't account for,
like a mother animal.

THE LIPSTICK

In my drawer
there's a tube of lipstick
I've had for years.
It's a cheap
brass-colored tube
with red lines around it.
The lipstick is greasy and pink
though little is left
but some goo in the bottom of the tube
and the strong smell
of the perfumed lipstick
I wore a long time ago
in a place I loved
but haven't seen since.
Once in a while
I take out the lipstick, smell it,
and feel stupidly happy.
No—better than happy,
as I did all that year
in a foreign country
with that smell
just under my nose.

THE GIFT

I love the book you gave me.
Did you think I didn't?
I don't squeal like people on game shows
or beauty contest winners,
but like a gibbon in a park zoo
I must take a gift off into a corner
to inspect it.
This is a fault, perhaps,
but I am a reserved person.
When pleasure, when joy
run through me,
it is as if I had stepped
into a fast green current.
I must go slowly to keep my balance.
Please understand
how happy I feel tonight
sitting here in bed, reading—
the rough brown jacket,
the green cloth cover,
the type which is *Olympus,*
a version of *Trump Mediaeval,*
the beautiful words
of this book you gave me.

I LOOK AT THESE PICTURES

I look at these pictures of you as a child
and think how strangely the past still exists
but on the other side of a gelatin window.
It gives me a strange, pleasurable feeling
to see you there when I didn't know you,
a little boy in a white shirt with an ornate collar,
rather nautical, and a double row of buttons down the front,
a pair of dark short pants, the cowlick in your hair
distinctive and difficult as it is now
when I cut your hair too short
and it stands on end for a week or two
until it gets long enough to lie down again.

And this one—you before forty, a teacher
with more hair and fewer lines in your face than now,
but with the same brows and deep set eyes, the same
nose with an odd crease down it. When I look at these pictures
I almost feel I could slip a hand in, around to the back,
and pull you out of them.

And here is a picture of me, a long time before you knew me.
I was with someone else then
but you can't see him because he's holding the camera.
I am standing on the Acropolis in Athens, wearing
sunglasses and a scarf, a black cotton coat over
a gold sweater I knit myself on the way across the country
riding in someone else's old Packard in order to get to Montreal
to catch a freighter to Europe. And I am wearing
a green cotton skirt that was one of two skirts

which were all I had to wear that year. They were enough.
I am standing on the Acropolis in front of the caryatids
of the Parthenon, a Doric temple of Athena, 5th c. BC.
It was 1963, in April.
The caryatids have suffered since then
from acid rain and are no longer there.
They have been put away in a museum
and the originals replaced with copies, like the David
in Florence, which you can see in more than one place
and never be sure you've seen the real one.
This me in the picture, in the sunglasses and black cotton coat,
the funny high heels and the brown cotton stockings
like ones the village women wore, is really me,
the me I was and still am.
But look how thin I was.
And how beautiful the caryatids.
We are all facing the same direction.
I am trying to pass as one of the family.

THE WOMAN IN
THE MOUNTAINS

for Alice

The woman in the mountains
makes me a bed in her house,
assuages my hungers
with grapefruit, tea, and poetry,
shows me an old jade tree
and art on the walls.
Offhandedly, as if by habit, she remarks
on her unfinished house,
the carpenter her husband, the process
spanning years. Much is complete
but here and there
sub-floors are exposed,
windows half framed.
No house is really finished,
is my thought.
She invites me to look at her study.

Next morning, after a rainy night,
outside these broad bright windows
mists rise in the canyon, beautiful
the way Japanese woodcuts
are beautiful. These fir trees are giants.
One hundred views of a mountain,

sunlight on dripping forest.
Layers of light and shadow.

Alone in this private house
I climb the stairs to where she writes, see
plants clustered at windows,
piles and shelves of books,
papers on the desk scattered and stacked,
photographs of her beloved daughter.
All this life in progress.
A friend of my own heart
lives in this thankfully
unfinished world.

THE EXAM

Here I am, due for the annual probing.
I sit in the examination room
staring at the poster on the wall opposite,
a woman, cigarette in her right hand
her insides carefully laid open and labeled,
her hair a country and western big-hair silhouette.
The poster points out all the ways that smoking
can kill you: cancer here, cancer there.

I'm glad I quite smoking, I think it was
thirty five years ago.
I decided to trade smoking for other dangers,
pierced ears and birth control pills.
Etta Abrahams did the ears
with an ice cube for an anesthetic
and a needle out of my sewing kit.
She told me she'd done it before
so I trusted her.

Last night I dreamed about a boy
I'd gone to a dance with, fifty years ago.
He's dead now, but in the dream when I said,
"I thought you were dead," he replied,
"No, I'm still here." We laughed.
In the dream I felt happy.
I don't remember if he smoked.

Dying has been on my mind, not that I plan
on dying soon, but the lawyer said I need
to make a will, and I've put off doing it
because I don't know how to go about it,

so I bought a little kit, "Last Will and Testament"
with directions and a CD. It's odd in a way
to set down directions, to keep running
your material life after you die.

I wonder when that doctor is going to come in here
and get it over with. I get good care.
She's thorough, good at recommending
specialists, takes her time talking
about whatever's on my mind this year.
Her eyes are so blue, maybe she has blue contacts.
I saw her once shopping at Safeway, wearing a blue coat
the color of her eyes. She told me she lives
in that house I drive by every day
on my way to work. Seeing your doctor
in the crackers and cookies aisle at Safeway
and driving by her house,
is like running into my students in the *real world*.
She lives in a nice house, though the yard is full of cars.
I remember the cars that used to sit in our yard
when I was with my first husband. He'd bring
them home with good intentions of fixing them up
but never got around to it. Instead he'd chop wood
and stack it around the cars to disguise the fact
that we had so many old cars in the yard,
all those woodpiles...
People would come to our house and say,
"My, you've got a lot of firewood."
Once I lifted the hood on one of the cars, an old green
Plymouth station wagon, and a rabbit jumped out.
It had built a nest on the engine block.

That woman with the cigarette in the poster
somehow looks like a woman you'd see in a western bar,
the silhouette of her hair surrounding that
exposed head full of sinuses, nasal passages,
roots of teeth, a brain and eyeballs,
one hand holding that cigarette, the other on her hip.
If she weren't opened up that way
she might look like Loretta Lynn or Tammy Wynette.
Cancer, cancer, cancer, it can pop up anywhere—
worse if you smoke.

Time goes by. I wonder why
I dreamed of that boy after all these years
and what happened to him? I just know
someone told me he'd died. I hear the doctor now
outside the door. Another year. I think I'm healthy.
About that dance we went to, that boy and I,
it's funny—I can't remember if we kissed or not.

ANOTHER BIRTHDAY

Where does middle-age stop
and old age begin?

I am making my way
through the architecture
of the ages.

There goes Chartres.
Hello Stonehenge.

LOVE OVER SIXTY

Here's to the slippery and the stiff,
the biscuit and the fish,
the tight and the loose and the in/between.
Here's to remembering and looking forward
and the size of the moment,
the round and the soft and the saggy of the moment,
the wrinkles like a well used map of the moment.

Treasure the blur of seeing up close
and the distance in the lens.
Blessed be the furry and the fuzzy,
the hairless and the taut,
the slow and the fast and whatever comes next.
Let the race be to the leisurely.
The silk and the wool and the cotton,
the pills and the table, the magazine.

The now and the then and more often,
the wrinkled sheet, the coffee in bed,
the toenail and the armpit,
the thumb joints and the arches,
the bathroom and the leaky flashing around the chimney,
the sound of the refrigerator humming
like an old, old song,
and all the rest of it.

THE AMAZING
71-YEAR-OLD HUSBAND

a love poem

I used to be strong, he says,
after spending the day pressing wine,
lifting the vats of fermented purple juice,
pouring it all into the press,
winding the screw down against the mast,
funneling the liquid into five gallon carboys,
then lifting and carrying each one into the wine room.
Last week he chopped wood,
and then plowed the garden for fall.
I used to be strong, he says again with a sigh.
Silly husband. Amazing husband.

UNEXPECTED VISIONS

For Monica and Kass
In the week of the rare transit of Venus

The badger peering from his den on Steens mountain,
swans flying low in fog over the house,
the tufted bobcat walking along our road,
turning to stare, then gliding
into high grass by the neighbor's pond,
an otter swimming along the rocky shore
of Sucia Island in the San Juans
on a hot day in July, air smelling of seawater
and the forest duff.

A red moose by the road
in the mountains of Utah, browsing.
She lifts her head to see us pass.
The Monarch butterfly out of its habitat,
nectaring on the butterfly bush
outside our window in western Oregon,
clouds of white pelicans forming a double helix
in hot air over Malheur Lake in the high desert,
and the same day, pelicans in a fishing circle,
thrashing their black tipped wings, closing in,
driving the fish to the center and pulling them up
with their tremendous beaks.
The road runner swiftly passing at a park
outside Tucson, the black-crowned night heron
clinging to a bush in Harney County,
the whale breaching off shore
near Cascade Head, then turning
and breaching again,

the baby humming birds gaping in their nest
in the blackberry thicket, the new-fledged owlets
downy and white in the willow grove
in Fields, Oregon, the sand hill cranes
doing their dance, the cicada with its wings
still folded, its eyes pink and new,
its body green as grass, before changing...

You have to be there at the right moment.
You have to be there.

Part Two

MATTERS OF FAITH

When I drive on the freeway
or especially on a four lane road
with no divider
and travel believing
that no one will come across the center line
and run into me
it is almost like believing
in something bigger than us all:
a comet keeping to its path,
the continuing power of the electric company,
an oak tree not falling
when you walk under it,
God even.

NEAR FRENCHGLEN

In early October, near Frenchglen,
the whistling swans maneuver in pairs
on the ponds and lakes of Harney county.
We get there late, this year, for cranes.
Day before, over a thousand Sandhill cranes
left for California, their winter grounds.
According to my bird book,
hunters shoot them in season. Not here,
but in California.

Sandhill Cranes mate for life, as do the swans.
Life for a crane
may mean fifty years or more.
Cranes, *the color of ash or wet sand*,
with red-capped heads.
They go along, eight years or so,
migrations, transmigrations, feeding,
jostling, flocking, stalking the small
frogs and other items of their menu,
without so much as laying an egg.
Then, all of a sudden, comes the
trumpeting call.
Love, the rhythmic dance, takes them.
Love.
Smack of two halves joining,
if only cranes. *If only?*
What am I saying? Amazing cranes.
To mate for life, taking that grand
implacable risk of being incomplete
without the other
in a world that shoots cranes.

STEENS MOUNTAIN

Peter French ranched in the Blitzen valley, above which
Steens mountain rises. The road goes up
ten thousand feet. We stop at 9,700,
walk to the edge
of the escarpment
overlooking Mickey Hot Springs
and the Alvord Desert. Even at this height
plants flower: lupine, miniaturized,
as if in a transistor something crystallized and blossomed;
clover, dandelions, and lichen, green and gold and red
as Christmas. Steens Mountain gorges
are textbook examples of glacial action,
notably, Kiger gorge, upon whose curved sides
bright aspens cling and twinkle
along the timberline.

On the road to the top, before the last
aspens thin and disappear,
we stop to watch a grove, all white and gold,
fluttering in the autumn light.
Along a dirt trail, I see
a badger rise from its den.
Astounded and thin of breath, I hurry to tell the others.
They ask, "How do you know it's a badger?"
"*Wind in the Willows*," I tell them.
(Once I knew olive trees, first seeing them live,
from paintings by Van Gogh.)
When we return, badger obliges us all
with another look, pulling to full height
in the opening of his burrow as if to assess
what planet we've come from. Bill climbs an aspen,
looking, I tell him, more ape than human,

as he swings, jouncing along the slender trunk
of the limber tree. John and Lynn, Pete and Kareen
and I, envoys from Planet X, march toward badger.
He stands his ground.
"Here I am. Get a good look.
Spread the word. This is Badger's Mountain."

Later, back in the valley, we pass the spot where
Peter French was murdered by a competing rancher.
French developed the French ranch, 138,000 acres.
Not enough room for both of them.
Swallows nest by the hundreds
in the old round barn Peter French used
for summer camp and bringing in horses.

Late afternoon, we walk
past meadowlarks and lizards, across the causeway
onto crumbled blacktop of the old road.
Today, Malheur Lake and Harney
have joined to become one lake,
a geological event that has not occurred
for millions of years, but did at least
a couple times before. A ranch house
sinks beneath the lake waters
and old barbed wire draws crazy lines
between "my water" and "your water".
We go as far as we can, over
the crumbled road, slimy gravel lapped
by the rising water on either side,

and peer toward distant white birds
we cannot distinguish.
"Come here," we call, wanting
so much to see what birds they are,
wanting to know which names they occupy
in this landscape of coyote, mule deer, whistling swans,
herons, cranes, egrets; in this landscape
of badger (do not forget badger).
We climb the ruin of a gate where someone's driveway
had been before the lake's rise, slipping
on the wet road that sinks and leaves us standing
still too far away. "Come here, come here, white things,"
we plead. And then the things unsettle, spread wings
amazingly, pull themselves up, in motion
out on the still lake. Rising, a scarf
circling, the birds come toward us, wide
wings moving with pterodactyl strangeness.

It is almost frightening to get what we want, but here
they come, as we have pleaded, toward us,
definitely toward us. They are
great snowy white pelicans with black wing tips,
a flock of twenty, thirty, flying toward us.
Across that great, unexpected lake,
they come to where we stand, at the end of the flooded road,
and call us with their coming. As we stare up,
they circle once, twice, low, seem to inspect us too,
on that flooded road we can travel no further.
Then—thank you, white pelicans with black wing tips,

thank you pelicans, giving us this favor—they
wheel once more and leave us, go back
to the far side of a lake
that measures its pleasure to come and go
in millions of years.

At night we climb coyote hill
to listen for the far off yipping.
We study the patterns of stars
over the Blitzen valley, Frenchglen,
and Steens, no, Badger's Mountain.

STINK ANT

I am watching television,
a nature show. I don't know
which one it is—about the jungles
of South America.
I'm feeling comfortable,
a wool blanket tucked around my knees,
slippers on, cocoa,
the usual securities.

A stink ant appears on the screen,
a solitary stink ant the commentator calls it,
whose neighborhood is the jungle floor.
There it goes—ta da ta da, happy stink ant.
Till high above a mushroom shoots its spore
which lands on the ant's poor head
and gives its brain a little spin.
Then all it wishes to do is climb
a lofty blade of grass.

Now, high above the jungle floor,
the stink ant rants and raves and roars
and clamps itself immovable
upon that stem and dies.
The stink ant conveniently dead,
a little bouquet of mushrooms
grows out of the vase of its head.

Thank God for my blanket,
my cocoa and my couch,
my healthy lack of ambition
in my television watching condition.
At times like these it's easy to imagine
the desire to get up in the world
is nothing more than a fungus infection.

THE NAKED RAT

The Portland zoo is exhibiting a naked rat.
It's pink and wrinkled
and naturally has no hair.
The zoo says the naked rat
always attracts big crowds.
I wonder why. He's very small
and unimportant looking.
Maybe people are
just happy to see
some other creature besides themselves
naked.

Poor naked rat.
Make him a little suit
and put him in it.
Then we'll recognize him for what he is,
our naked little brother.

THE MAN FROM THE PAST VISITS THE PRESENT

The man who comes up the road
is tall and thin and elderly, white-haired
with glasses, doesn't look anything like
the boy he says he was when he lived here
on our farm, eighty years ago.

Fascinated, wanting to draw the missing figures
in my picture of this landscape,
I ask him about the house, the well, the trees.
He says he has never loved
any other place so well as this one
where he lived when he was two,
and which his family kept
for a retreat, till he was eighteen.

He remembers Sunday picnics,
the community of Bohemian farmers
who came together on Sundays
to play music, eat from picnic baskets.
He remembers picking almonds from these trees—
is it possible these three, spindly old trees
bringing forth eight or ten nuts each year
are those? In photos he shows me I see
the familiar contour of our mountain,
much older than almond trees or any
growing thing on the place. And there
are the Bohemians, the family and friends,

men in hats and suits sitting on the hill
above where the vineyard is now, once
an orchard of peaches, plums. Their musical
instruments are cocked across their laps.
The women's dresses are long, down to their ankles.

He offers a picture of his mother
who, he tells us, stood on the rim
of the deep well his father dug by hand,
a cistern twenty feet deep or more to hold rainwater.
As his father filled buckets with dug dirt
his mother would pull them up from the dark hole.
We still use that cistern in the heat of summer
to water the plants in pots along the porch.

We have a lot in common, this man and I,
knowing how hard the ground is here, how dry
and ungiving except for the Oregon white oaks,
the savannah grasses, the wild rose, poison oak,
snowberries.

EVERY YEAR

When they are two or three weeks old
the lambs begin to gambol as if
no other lambs had ever gamboled:
leaping in the air with a joyful twitch,
kicking their legs, and running
in a little herd, back and forth,
back and forth, exhilarated
as if they believe
they have invented
gamboling.

And every year they discover
the two foot bole growing from the side
of the oak tree's trunk
like a woody wart.
They climb on it, pushing
one another off
as if they had invented pushing off.

And every year, I call to my husband,
Look at the lambs.
They're playing king of the hill,
and I laugh as if I'd never before
seen them do such a thing.

THE DEAD MAN'S FOOT
September 2004

On the last day of summer
the Dead Man's Foot comes up in the vineyard,
woody and brown and scattering a dark powder
when I touch it: *pisolithus tinctorius*.
We've never seen it on our place before.
I wonder what this means,
but every year is *unusual* in the country.
In July, unfamiliar orchids appeared on the west pasture:
lady's tresses, and something else a creamy white.
Now in September, holes in the ground where orchids were.
Does this mean that skunks have feasted?

In the woods, acorns drop by the thousands,
more than we've seen in seventeen years, like cicadas,
but the grapes are poor, the harvest scant.
Luckily we have wine from past autumns.

And now this dead man's foot appears.
Jack the Mushroom Man says:
"the species epithet refers
to its use as a dye for wool...it is a good
mycorrhizal associate of various trees."
He asks what trees are growing
in its immediate vicinity.
His specific knowledge is impressive.
My knowledge is so generalized.
I consider: oak, hazel, walnuts, the vines....

What I do know is, all these acorns
tapping the roof, rapping the car, hitting us on our heads,
all this abundance tells us: plant oak trees this year.
So we scatter them beyond the woods
to assist them in their Diaspora.
Grow, I tell them. Grow.
The dead man's foot wiggles its toes.

PLEA TO SORE FEET

Left, left—I left my wife and forty-nine children
in starving condition without any gingerbread,
Right, right, do you think I did right?

Feet you are sometimes a pain,
pretending to be so tough,
modest as dog shit and proud as bumble bees,
yet succumbing to plantar fascitis
and crooked toes like a fainting Victorian.
Is it your nature to be contradictory?
You proceed like the waddling bandit,
this way, that way: recalcitrant twins, sorry soldiers,
an army of two falling over yourselves
like Laurel and Hardy.

Is it because I have thoughtlessly danced upon you
as if you were merely the rude mechanicals,
serving my Titanian self, Quasimodo to my Esmeralda?
So what if I boogied carelessly,
accepting your plebian servitude,
perhaps without sufficient gratitude?
What do you expect? You were made for it.
You aren't sensitive fingers with opposable thumbs
even if you can pick up a pencil now and then
or, icy, shock a spouse awake and stretch
sometimes to click a switch.
You have your little tricks—ta-da!—
but you're feet. Your job is to hold me up.
Your purpose is transportation.

I know I have stubbed, sprained, scraped you
on gravel, stepped carelessly on thorns,
torn a tendon, broken a toe or two. Sor-ry!
But remember the times I dressed you
in black shiny tap shoes with grosgrain bows,
blue suede shoes and red ballet slippers,
cowboy boots, fancy socks,
and increasingly expensive Birkenstocks.
I have treated you to massages and sanded away calluses,
trimmed your horny nails, scrubbed away toe jam.
I have fondly caressed you with sweet smelling lotions,
patchouli, lavender, eucalyptus and rose,
emollient balms meant only for you, my feet.
So remember the good times.
We have come a long way,
don't quit on me now.

WET LAND

Wapato is blooming this month, *Sagittaria latifolia,*
"a round root the size of Hens eggs,"
favored as food by native inhabitants of Oregon,
once abundant around here.
Driving north I pass a pond full of Wapato
now blooming, the small white flowers
elevated on long stems
like spots of sunlight on shiny leaves.

Later, going south, I see the farmer
unloading drain pipe for the field at the curve.
It means he is going to put an end to the silver pools
that stand there in winter.
I know he is tired of farming,
wants to subdivide, build houses
at the bend of the road into town.
I feel a sigh of grief, thinking
I will no longer see that pond in winter.
The water will rush away
as if it were an unwelcome guest saving face,
pretending it has somewhere
more important to go.

Once in the Wapato marsh I saw a red mare
standing in water up to her chest. Her neck arched
as she pulled wet weeds with her mouth.
I never go past there without hoping
to see her again, to see the red horse
up to her broad chest, mouthing weeds.

JANUARY 1 – SIGNS

Wind and rain again,
every day since Christmas.
Decided to drive to Fern Hill
to look for birds.
At the end of the driveway Bill noticed
the pickup tank was almost empty
so we drove two miles into Yamhill
to look for gas instead.
Stations all closed for New Year's Day.

Drove home again, got the dogs out
of the truck, loaded them
into the station wagon.
Drove to the end of the driveway,
realized this gas tank too
was almost empty.

Parked the car. Got the dogs out.
Decided we'd walk our own road, look
for the White-tailed Kite.
At the end of the driveway
a flock of eight swans came
from the direction of the vineyard,
flying low behind the scrub oaks
and out of the wind.
They floundered, then turned south,
grew small, disappeared.

Wind came harder when we got to the
corner of Goodrich Road. The White-tailed Kite
was in its usual place

on the phone wire, but took off as we
approached, hovered in the wind, then
landed in the old walnut tree
on the neighbor's field.
Now trees were lashing back and forth
and branches were flying.
We decided we'd turn around.

At the bottom of our place, water
in the culvert sounded like a great falls.
We went over the fence, unleashed the
dogs and walked up through the wild
apples and the pines Bill planted last
year to satisfy the tax guy.
Bear scat from October had turned
brown and crumbled,
now just sodden apple peels in piles.
Rain had melted a twist of coyote dung
to mud and hair—in that matter we saw,
strangely woven, skin of a garter snake
and the leathery toe of a chicken.
Our Barred Rock disappeared last week.

We went uphill, out of the woods and
through the vineyard where water ran clear.
The dogs, wet and sleek as seals,
romped happy to be off leash
and coming home.
Near the house, I slipped in mud
and fell, hit my shoulder,
the back of my head.

Two empty gas tanks, mud everywhere,
a bump on my head.
I went in, took two aspirin,
ran the bathtub full
of hot water with bubble bath,
dropped my clothes, got in,
lay there breathing steam
and daydreaming for an hour
as I soaked mud out of my hair.

One Kite. Eight swans.
Chicken toe.
Snake skin.
Black dogs leaping.
Mud and wind.
Bear scat. Bear scat.
This is the way
the year begins.

CAT ON EGGS

Gigi the barn cat, sixteen years old,
has taken to sitting on eggs
the hens lay in hiding places
between bales of hay.
They're warm, and she
loves warmth for her old cat bones.

Our chickens—the red hen, the Barred Rock,
the Araucanas, and the black Australorp—
lay eggs, then wander off
to look for vermin in the barn debris
while the cat, opportunist as she is,
waits for them to leave, climbs on the nest,
curls and sleeps there.

I pull the eggs,
green, blue, pink, and brown,
out from under the soft fur of the cat's belly,
warm eggs in my hands.

ON CHARACTER

Taking a class in Chinese calligraphy

I make the characters awkwardly,
my hand and forearm poised
above the rice paper,
the brush balanced just so: pinky
and next finger
behind the bamboo stem,
pointer and middle before it.
The thumb, a counterbalance
locks them in.

A meditative process
the teacher calls it, slow, thoughtful.
I cover my pages with strokes for
rock, mountain, forest, tree…
As I perform the exercise
I notice my fingers are
like a weaving: the stem of the brush a warp
against the weft of digits.
One practices to make the hand
as it moves over the paper
an extension of thought,
or non-thought, or character.

The teacher looks over my shoulder
and points to the characters
I have drawn. *In this one*, he says,
you are a little hurried. Impatient.
But this one is better.
It is balanced, considered, upright.
I feel a small childish glow

of pleasure in being
balanced, considered, upright,
if only for one character.

Is this penmanship?
I wonder. My penmanship,
a slightly military word
like marksmanship or
sportsmanship,
has never been
praiseworthy in conventional ways,
though I recognize my handwriting
as mine and even like it
when it is reduced
to abstraction,
writing as design.

What is so mysteriously pleasing
in curves and lines of black ink?
I only know I like seeing them,
and that the word character,
in this context, pleases me:
the character of a character
being the character of the character
who is writing
the character.

Soon this line of thought
reduces the word *character* to salad.
But my hand continues
moving down the page,
as I practice this unfamiliar language
for the familiar: characters for
tree, mountain, rock, forest,
water, flower, east, cloud,
the character for form, for something,
and my favorite
this beautiful character
which means empty,
or maybe nothing.

ONCE UPON A HORSE

I've often wished I'd learned to ride
when I was a child, but my experience with horses
was a circle of dull ponies at carnival
plodding round and round in harness,
like an antique mill. Their rough
sweet-smelling hides chafed my thighs
exposed by the short dress—I was six or so.
And once a neighbor lifted me up high
onto the back of a fine bay
he led up and down the street
for the amusement of us kids.
I don't know where that horse came from.
The neighbor was a judge, at least
people called him Judge. I used to watch
his sons and the sons' friends, boys older than I was,
running through their yard, playing war
at night. From my high window I could see
where each was hiding, better than they could,
as they ran shooting one another
with wooden guns or throwing
pine cone grenades. A silent spy, a girl,
I'd kneel on the upstairs hallway floor
peering through the narrow crack I'd left
between shade and sill, with the light off
so no one would see me there.
There was a real war going on, I knew,
on the other side of the world.
I was happy to be on our side
where children had enough to eat

and bombs did not explode.
We didn't have a car then, because
of wartime gas shortage, just
the company car dad brought home
from his work as telephone man,
but mom and dad both had motorcycles
for a while. A Harley was his steed,
and for her, an Excelsior, lightweight and quiet.
Dad took me on the Harley once or twice,
a noisy beast, but I preferred the Excelsior,
a slim bike mother could manage.

We never had horses ourselves, though I knew
dad had a horse when he was young.
I'd seen the photos of dad with Gypsy,
the brown and white pony he used to ride
to school in Kansas when he was a kid.
On winter Sundays, he told me,
he'd ride Gypsy to a country crossroad
to meet his friends. Boys and girls,
they all had horses—lucky! All day
they'd ride, racing their ponies in the snow.

Imagining this, I'd play at being a horse,
whinny, toss my mane, paw the ground,
but never had a chance to really ride one
till the judge showed up that day.
It was just one afternoon. The boys
quit playing war to watch, and the judge

took each of us in turn and walked
the horse up and down the block.
It was a great afternoon, better than a carnival,
but after dark the boys went back to war.

That's it. My big horse story.
I still like horses, to look at that is,
but you know, when you grow up
without getting used to a thing
it's not like you can go back. I'm not young.
I'm afraid to get up on something that tall.
Still, when I drive my twelve miles to work
I notice horses all along the way.
There are two appaloosas just outside town,
white and gray with spotted rumps. I've watched them
since they were foaled. And the ponies across the way
with their winter coats, dark, shaggy, and steaming.
On the other side of the valley, that neighbor
sometimes brings his Morgan out.
I can feel it with my knees.
When I see a sign go up: *horse for sale*,
I sometimes think, "What if? What if?"

A MILLION SPLINTERS
OF GLASS

You say to someone, "How's it going?"
They answer:
"Ah, I had a root canal Tuesday,
and then there's this war."
You say to someone, "How are you?"
They answer:
"My clutch went out,
and then there's this war."
You say to someone, "How've you been?"
They answer:
"Doctor says I've got to have
a hysterectomy,
and then there's this war."
Though it's not in proportion
I know what they mean.
The neighbor's dog
mauled one of my sheep last week,
blood and wool all over.
I followed the trail of her wool,
lustrous white wool
that warmed her through winter,
that could have been a blanket or a sweater,
that could have been something
warm and useful and beautiful,
now bloody and dirty and ruined,

strung through the blackberry thicket,
on the ground under the apple trees,
hooked on the barbed wire fence.
The vet, the sheriff—
everybody in the driveway
when I got home,
I followed the trail of the ewe's terror,
sick at the waste and the pain of it.
All week I'm doctoring
my chewed-up sheep
and then—to top it off
here comes this war.

I BRAKE FOR BUMPERSTICKERS

A woman advocating that we
*practice random kindness
and senseless acts of beauty*
passes me on the curve
coming into the no-passing zone
throwing mud on my windshield
and further flattening
a dead skunk.

FIGURE

The little god
sits cross legged
on the shelf above my computer,
Robes collapse
on his shoulders
and expose his bare belly.
He sits on grass and
leans against a rock,
fan in one hand,
face like a happy baby.

I carried him here
from a junk store on the Oregon coast.
When I asked where he came from,
the proprietor leaned over the counter
and told me a story
of an old woman
who left the little god there,
a woman who had traveled far
and at the end of her life
came to our western land.

Women do that,
pick up little gods
and carry them through the world.
When the women put them down
these clever gods
usually find someone else,
like me,
to take them home.

It pleases me to see him sitting there
between the router
and the speakers
of my computer.
Even if he is just plastic,
he makes me feel
I am one of the chosen,
one of the lucky ones.

INSOMNIA I: SUMMER

Hello Margaret, almost done
with August—month of an emperor,
month of crickets,
month of forest fire sunsets.
You should have seen the one this evening,
the color of fuchsias, silk sunset
out of *Gone with the Wind* or *Wizard of Oz*.
And now what stars there are are red too,
the sky's that hazy
from the burns down south.
What if we always had red stars? I wouldn't like it,
to miss those diamond lights
clear as water in the Coast Range creeks.

My sister called, said she couldn't sleep
last night. I couldn't either.
Then my daughter said she couldn't sleep.
Running through all our heads, those end of summer blues
and reds. My sister
got up at three a.m. to drink a bourbon,
her kids slept on the couch and rug, restless in the heat.
That day it had been 105 degrees and still was hot.
Her husband thought it was time to get up and go to work.
Walking out, getting dressed, he said, "What's going on here?
I smell bourbon. What the heck? It's only four a.m.!"
Telling me this she laughed but she was sleepy.
Me, I didn't try a drink,
always a mistake with insomnia in my experience.
Can't turn off the white nights simply as that.
I just think. And think. Small issues rise
to trouble me and grow large. Next morning I wonder
why night glooms seem so compelling until the sun comes up.

My mother tells me, a friend's daughter is in a coma
from overdose of drugs. No one knows why
or what happened,
whether it was prescription or mistaken recreation.
I don't know where she is, how to call her, or even
which daughter for sure. Imagine a coma, a spell
of sleep like Sleeping Beauty or Snow White
with the apple in her throat, or Poe's character in
The Fall of the House of Usher—Madeline—
they thought was dead but she revived and walked
out of her tomb. In the movies they show a line
across a screen—that's supposed to be the brain without
excitement, thought, consciousness, without even a dream
to jiggle the line of existence, and there's a beep
like a car or truck that's set to make
a sound to warn you backing up.

The month comes down upon me like a wind
in some wild canyon somewhere,
Steens, Juntura, some other place like that I've been
at end of summer. And there's richness to it too,
the color of the sun is red each night, the sheep look good,
the sunlight makes an aura on their wool that's like
the rim of light on that far off hill at six o'clock.
Insomnia only lasts, for me, a week or so
and then I'm back to drowsy habits.
Send me your poems.
Write and tell me how you are.
It's good to be able to sleep
when you need to, isn't it.

INSOMNIA II: WINTER

To bed once, then up again two hours later,
and no sleep yet, I wonder
whether to keep trying or just go
to bed and let the stories
run through my head.

Once I slept at the top of a house
with a cold stairway below
and the parental injunction
to keep me in bed
when the thing that doesn't sleep
came looking for me.

Now, sixty years later and well grown,
I have only myself to answer to
when I can't sleep. Dear husband
rolls over, snores, doesn't notice,
so well he performs
his early-to-bed, early-to-rise routine.

The black and white dogs keep me company,
move from beside the bed to my office
where I turn the computer on
and let its blue light shed a little comprehension,
electronic en-lightenment.
It makes a white place
for the voices in my head to go.

Outside, last week's snow
is finally melting, ghost of snow rising
as a blue fog that obscures the landscape.
All day I could barely see beyond the
pasture fence, no view of the mountains,
not even the oak grove, or the back
of the neighbor's house in the hollow.
Tonight, not even fog, just gleaming black
outside the glass.

I've been waiting
for a night to get the telescope out
and look at stars,
Venus, Saturn, and Mars are supposed to
be good this month. But only the moon appears,
and even that white face barely shows
through the mist and clouds these winter nights.
January passes. Winter passes.
Maybe it will soon be clear
and seeing all, like a new moon,
I'll sleep.

MOONS AT 9:30 PM

Dark enough now
to look at Jupiter
with the little telescope.
Four moons visible.
I call the grandchildren
to see it
but they jiggle the telescope
and I can't get it back.
Mosquitos are gathering.
What is near is good also.
Before going inside
we'll take a quick peek
at our big white moon,
our consolation moon.

50TH CLASS REUNION

Our faces are turned up into the wind.
Some of us are fat now, some of us are not.
Our hair is gray or sparse,
or black or blonde or red
according to the latest chemistry.
Some of us have died: the boy I went
to the senior prom with, the boy I went
to the Sadie Hawkins dance with, the girl
who was one of my best friends.
Two of us have committed murders
and live in prison; one sends a poem.

We were loud and strong.
We always won our games.
Once a Pirate always a Pirate, is our motto.
We stand at the edge of a planked surface.
Beyond the weather stained boards
the water is the color of aquamarine, like the stone
in a ring I lost years ago, maybe
fifty years ago. Dark little peaks
stirred up by ocean breezes
move across the water's surface.
The wind lifts our hair from our round old faces.
The other side of the bay is not visible.

Part Three

THE ROUNDS

How do you speak to the tree in the field?
With the voice of a red-winged blackbird.

And here I am in the pasture
making my daily rounds.
Every day is different, something new,
something with a face like silk
and eyes from a science fiction movie,
something with breath
like wind over yellow winter grass,
something with teeth or mandibles or roots,
with egg sac, fur, or a stamen and pistil.

How do you greet frog spawn in the west pond?
With amazement and expectation.

One day ice crystals are flashing their blue lights,
the next an intimation of spring
in the changing color of lungwort,
in the vibrations of dark pools at
the base of oak trees.

Where is the rose hip hidden?
In the thorny stem, in the thread of its being.

MYSTERIES OF THE PICTURE BOX

1

James Thomas Robertson, my grandfather,
at age eighteen, wears a suit and tie.
The collar of his shirt has rounded corners.
The tie itself is light-colored and has
a tie tack or a bit of design, not sure which.
His face is handsome but sad and serious
under the curly, brushed back hair.
I imagine his hair reddish like my father's.
Thirty four years later, a little past fifty,
in 1939, the year I was born,
he will die of a sudden fever,
possibly from encephalitis.
Death was mysterious in those days.
Still is.

2

In this one grandfather sits on his horse.
A rifle dangles from the pommel of his saddle,
points toward the earth. A coil of rope flops
on the horse's shoulder. Grandfather's pants
are felted wool. He wears
a wide, high belt and collarless buttoned shirt.
In his broad-brimmed hat, he looks the perfect cowboy.
Next to him, the hired man, Sweet Pea,

sits on a mule and wears a sombrero.
Sweet Pea too is draped with gear, rifle in his hands.
What were they up to? The guns, the ropes, the horses?
Behind them, a line of willows,
and through the branches of the trees,
the eternal flat line of Kansas
like a stopped heart.

3

Grandpa looks happy in this one.
The horse is rearing for the picture,
and Grandfather's shirt is dark, collared.
He is wearing chaps and his hat is white, naturally,
for my Grandfather was surely the good guy.
The horse's tail sweeps the ground
and its hooves are white as Grandpa's hat.

4

Together my grandparents,
Grace and James, stare out of this picture.
James, a shy man it seems,
looks slightly to the camera's right.
I cannot see into his eyes.
I won't be born for years.
Grace looks at me directly.
I will know her. She
will live briefly to know me.
He will not.

5

The whole family is in this picture
and everyone is pleased with the new car.
You can tell by the jaunty way their hands
sit on their hips. Even dad at seven or eight,
dressed for the occasion in knee-length black pants
and a little jacket, a boy-size necktie and big cap
cocked over one eye, stands with arms akimbo
as if a desire for action, speed and travel
were being translated into an unnatural pause.
The camera records this moment of awe.
James, Grace, and the boys—
the four of them stare at the camera
and stand jauntily in front of the new vehicle,
its sleek long hood like the muzzle of a dog
or the body of the century's newest animal.

LIFE MAP: CLATSKANIE

Here is Clatskanie, the town
where I learned to read when I was four.
The old library was a house at the top of town.
This, said mother, *is the library.*
They have books you can read.
I inhaled the sweet, dry smell,
recognized my natural atmosphere.

That was our house.
I watched from the sunroom one night
as across town the high school burned.
The pear tree in the yard—
can it be the same tree?
After sixty years it's not much bigger—
maybe in time some things grow smaller.

This is the crossing where Maisy,
my pretty cocker spaniel,
was hit by a car,
ran to my lap, and died.
On that hill was Canham's house.
Francis raised chickens
and gave me a chick to raise once.

Upstairs in this brick building
is where my brother was born. I stayed
with our friends the Starrs,
Helen and Dr. Starr and their children,

Billy, Louanne, and Jim,
while mother enjoyed
her leisurely ten day confinement.
Helen's duck and dumplings were favorites
—Paul hunted, Helen cooked. I liked
the swift and tidy way, nurse fashion,
she mitered corners of bed sheets.
Next door to the Starrs were the Steeles
and their greenhouse.
I learned to draw pears and apples from watching
a girl paint fruit on pots there.

Stretched on a blanket in Starrs' back yard
I first read *Little Women*
the summer after first grade,
and sometimes sat in the play room reading
volumes of Nancy Drew
passed on from the Evensons
whose children were grown.

Downtown was Saville Dixon's drugstore
with ice cream cones—strawberry,
pistachio, black walnut—the Piggly Wiggly,
its frosty locker with a smell of meat,
the bakery on the same side of the street
as Jackie's father's tavern,
the candy shop where a girl named Willy,
cheeks pink, white-blonde hair gleaming,
weighed out and sold
magnificent blocks of rocky road candy.

There is the park we walked by,
Louanne, Billy, and I,
on our way to school
and where we saw a giant snake once—
we thought it had escaped
from the carnival with fire eaters and jugglers
that had been there the week before.
Our parents said it was just a vine.
I say it was a snake.

During the war, Father was
the telephone man of Clatskanie.
They sent him back from the draft
because he was the only one. It was up to him
to keep everything connected,
including the ammunition dump outside town.
When they called at odd hours
we'd drive out, Mom, Dad, and me,
and park at the gate. Inside was secret
so Mom and I waited in the truck
while Dad went in and fixed the trouble.

On the dike land, smell of mint fields
freshened and beckoned
from Earle Chartrey's farm.
At home our phone had a handle
to get the operator. If there was a siren
Dad would crank the handle, and say,
"Hello Central, Kansas here. Where's the trouble?"
Central always knew.
Sometimes I saw Central

when I went to work with dad.
She'd humor me with conversation
if she wasn't busy plugging cords in,
connecting everyone.

It was my town and I knew it all
for even though I was young and small
children ran free then.

Best of all was the river
where we picnicked spring,
summer, and fall. I'll never forget
the molasses smell of baked beans,
pickle and egg odors of potato salad,
fried chicken and hot dogs,
scents and sounds of the slough
where the boathouse floated
on log pontoons
blackened with mildew.
An outboard motor took us
between close banks
till we reached the river,
then wind picked up and sails filled
with a shiver. I sometimes rode
with Louanne
in the front hatch of Starrs' boat. We let
waves blow spray into our faces
as we sailed to the river side
of Wallace Island.

There everyone spent the day playing.
Sometimes there were boat races
or treasure hunts. In August 1945 a radio
on a big sailboat boat from Astoria
picked up the news: the war was over.
Our parents hugged and cheered
and the boys on the boat whooped
and jumped into the river.

I will always love the smell
of cottonwoods, wet sand,
odors of deck paint and boat gas,
wet canvas of life jacket
floating my skinny self.
I wanted to stay there forever,
to live on the island, to time
my heartbeat with the slap, slap, slap
of water lapping sand, like minutes passing.
Every moment was a tiny wave
pulling you under, holding you up.

Sailing back as dark came on
I lay in the boat and listened to the sounds:
up smack up smack run river run
up smack up smack run river run.
Growing sleepy, I fell into a dream
I may still be dreaming.

THE DAILY GLOOM

Why do I read the morning newspaper
with its litany of doleful events,
it's murders, wars, and bank closures?
Why keep up on current events—
the kidnappings, the accidents, the movie star divorces?
I scan these friable pages, the cheap paper,
the ink coming off on my fingers
buttery from my morning toast.
How foolish the human race,
how incomprehensible the stock market…
At least the comics are still here,
though my old friends,
Alley Oop, Smiling Jack, and Little Orphan Annie
have gone to the great colored pages in the sky.
No more Katzenjammers either.
But at least Dagwood is still with us.
God bless Dagwood.

Other than the comics,
the obituary page may be most cheerful of all.
I study the outdated picture of someone's smiling grandmother
in a cloche hat, the handsome young man in World War II uniform.
I skim the stories of lives now past
and check the dates to see who is older or younger than I am,
then turn to the science section
where something appears truly worth celebrating.
A comet named Lulin is passing.
a sweet, fuzzy light in a dark sky,
and we just might be able to see it.

I am always happy when comets appear,
as when I see a whale far out spouting
or a pileated woodpecker in August.
This is an opportunity not to be missed.
Drop everything. Let's go out to look at this comet
because it will not be back
for a thousand years
and who knows then,
what the world will be doing,
or who, if anyone, will be watching.

STILL DARK

Still dark when I reach
to turn the alarm off before it can ring.
December 2, 2008.
I drive to yoga class
where we do downward dog,
dancing warrior, warrior number two,
triangle, dancing triangle, the bridge. I don't like
the bridge. Finally we get
to the pigeon, a collapsed
kind of pose. Then Shavasana.

Thought I'd buy
Christmas chocolate for my brother
on the way home, but the handmade chocolate store
doesn't open till 11:00
so I go on to find Bill in the driveway
sliding a crate into the truck.
A barn owl, he says, injured, in the ditch.
He's off to meet an Audubon rep in Newberg.
The owl in shock looks pitiful. So light, so small
compared to the grand dignity
of looking down from high rafters, from flight.
He has wrapped it in towels to travel.
Can it survive? I ride along.

After we turn the owl over
to the woman with the same name as mine
we stop at the Newberg Panaderia for a donut.
Their donuts are better than other donuts.
The man behind the counter speaks Spanish.
The customers ahead of me
speak something that sounds Middle Eastern.

Might donuts be a common language?
I don't usually buy donuts
but if I pass the Panaderia it's hard not to stop
and I feel sad about the owl.
Donut comfort. But not enough.

All along the road we see raptors—
kestrels, Red-tails, a marsh hawk.
Back home a Red-tail flies up
from the vineyard and perches
at the top of a fir tree.
Do birds notice what happens to other birds?

Bill asks, should we call later
and ask about the owl?
I don't want to know if it dies, I tell him.
He says he will call the Audubon office anyway.
He won't tell me if it didn't make it.
Well, I say, then that will be obvious.
When he calls I hear him from the other room.
His voice drops so I know the owl died.
They tell him shock, hypothermia, dehydration,
they did their best...

After these few hours of light it's dark again.
I walk out to see the conjunction of the moon,
Venus, and Jupiter, like a festival in the sky.
In mythologies the dead sometimes rise
and turn into constellations. Orion the Hunter
will be up soon. I'd like to look and find
a tiny barn owl
sitting on Orion's shoulder.

CEREMONY

This tiny cabin in the clearing
surrounded by old trees
is barely shelter in a rainstorm,
leaks around the windows,
is shared with spiders. Now and then
a banana slug off course veers in,
lays its shining trail.

Mouse-nibbled comic books
go back thirty years at least
to kids lounging in the Mexican hammock
slung between alders,
legs braced to spread the cotton weave,
heads propped for reading
Archie, Betty, and Veronica,
Casper the Ghost, Richie Rich,
Green Lantern.

That fossilized seashell
from a Cape Blanco midden
has been sitting on the porch rail
since 1976. This bottle of homemade
blackberry wine on the high shelf—
vintage 1980?—
no one in their right mind will ever drink it.
Collar from a long gone dog
hangs from a nail on the wall.
There's a dusty baseball cap
and a sickle to clear the trail.
This place is a monument to the dust-covered
but not forgotten, to light and dark,
to smoke and mirrors,
to children growing up and having children.

Each summer we fill
the place with new life.
Haul out the Coleman stove, light
the propane lantern, beat down the grass,
clip back a year's growth of blackberry vines,
restock the outhouse with toilet paper
kept dry under a rusted coffee can,
sweep out spiders, webs, dead flies,
polish windows, plant tents in the clearing,
spread sleeping bags, rebuild in the woods
a village of kinship.

Then we go to the river, wade in,
and with voices cunning and persuasive
to those still on the rocky bank
we call out the pleasing lie:
"Come in, come in—it's not cold,"
And even the little ones do.
Like dragons, ritually washed in season,
we swim.

THE SAVING PLACE

I am doing a lazy breast stroke
in late August on the Sixes River,
when I see a yellow alder leaf
spin from its branch.

Minnows nibble my white legs.
The kingfisher chatters overhead
as he flies upstream and the ouzel
dips shyly in the rapids.

When vine maple shows red.
on the mountain
I will know it's time
to swim back to my other life.

Yet all year long I will lay my body
in the river of memory.
All through the coming winter
these waters will keep me afloat.

OCTOBER

Last week it was hot in the mountains.
Sunshine stepped over the tops of fir trees
like a long legged marionette,
then descended to where we gathered,
a union of peace and aspiration.

Friday in the last heat
thirty vultures floated over the hill top,
turning and turning sociably,
above the vineyard
before flying south.
This morning the rain is here
and one late vulture
circles low over the pasture
trying to catch a last thermal
to waft him up and south.

Grapes are not yet ripe enough for wine.
Tomatoes burst on wet vines.
The earth, too summer-hard to easily bury
the old sheep who died yesterday,
will soon be soft..
Cold. Fog. A drizzle.

This morning at 7 a.m.
I cannot see the Coast Range.
Like the last vulture of summer,
I am not ready for any of this.

OUT IN THE DARK

Out in the dark the air smelled good
like laundry hung in the sun all day.
But it was night and pitch black dark.

The little frogs in the woods
began to cheer, leading us on
through the dark oak trees.

The young dog ran ahead on the path.
The old dog shuddered and tried to keep up
but fell behind at every step.

At the bottom of the pasture in the little woods
we stopped a moment to smell the dark,
then climbed the hill with nothing on our minds

but going inside where the fire burned bright,
a dark scent hoarded against the light.

LIKE A BOOK OPENING

Like a book opening
spring comes back to the landscape,
yellow daffodils reminding me of Wordsworth,
narcissus reminding me of Ovid.

Blossoms on the plums
sweet and earthy like hemp
conjure Basho or William Carlos Williams.
Wild hazel, tasseling,
bursts into song about Yeats
and Wandering Angus.

A snake resting in the sun
is a letter from Emily Dickinson,
and the green leaves of grass,
the beautiful uncut hair...
in the sheep pasture,
tell me Whitman is back again.

What a literary landscape spring is.
You must write your life.

ACKNOWLEDGMENTS

Some of the poems in *Driving One Hundred* first appeared in the following. With appreciation for these publications and their editors:

Calapooya Collage: "In the Dark Room"
Cloudbank: "The Rounds"
Fireweed: "Near Frenchglen"
From Here We Speak, The Oregon Literature Series, OSU Press: "Stink Ant"
Gargoyle 54: "Love Over Sixty"
Hubbub: "When the Airplane Stopped"
Left Bank: "Driving One Hundred"
Media Weavers: Writers Northwest: "Like a Book Opening"
Northwest Magazine, The Oregonian: "The Mother"
Oregon Literary Review: "The Woman in the Mountains" and "Cat on Eggs"
Poets on Place, W. T. Pfefferle, Utah State University Press: "The Man from the Past Visits the Present"
Portland Magazine: "Blackboard"
Portland Review: "A Million Splinters of Glass"
Stone Country: "The Smell of Man"
The Bridge: "Hard Hitter"
Windfall: "Unexpected Visions," "Every Year," "the Dead Man's Foot," "Wet Land," "January 1—Signs," "Life Map: Clatskanie," and "Still Dark"

With thanks and appreciation: to Bill Siverly and Michael McDowell for carrying the *Windfall* banner of poetry; to the members of the Tabus, the Poultry Group, and the Poetry Circle for helping me fine-tune many of these works in a book of long making; and especially to my husband, William Beckman, my first and best reader, personal photographer, and vintner par excellence.

ABOUT THE AUTHOR

Barbara Drake's books and chapbooks of poetry include *Love at the Egyptian Theatre, What We Say to Strangers, Life in a Gothic Novel, Bees in Wet Weather, and Small Favors.* She is also the author of a memoir, *Peace at Heart: an Oregon Country Life,* and *Writing Poetry,* a widely used college textbook. Her writing appears in numerous literary magazines and anthologies. *Peace at Heart* was an Oregon Book Award finalist in 1999.

Born in Kansas, she moved with her parents to Oregon as a small child and grew up in Coos Bay on the southern Oregon coast. She earned her B.A. and M.F.A. degrees from the University of Oregon, and subsequently lived in Michigan for sixteen years where she taught at Michigan State University before returning to Oregon to teach at Linfield College from 1983 until her recent retirement. The author and her husband live on a small Yamhill County farm in the foothills of the Oregon Coast Range.

She has driven across the country more times than she can count, but tries to observe the posted speed regulations.

Praise for other books by the author:

What We Say to Strangers
"Reading Barbara Drake for the first time, I felt no stranger. She spoke straight to me, and said truth." —Ursula LeGuin

Love at the Egyptian Theatre
"She is a master of transforming the everyday (American) into a music that only those with the New Ears will be able to hear. . . strong and inventive and bold..." —Diane Wakoski

"This is a single-poet collection that stands head and shoulders above others." —*Library Journal*

Peace at Heart: An Oregon Country Life
"Conjuring with a poet's grace and a wise heart, she illustrates our human connection to earth and sky. This is how we are meant to live, one imagines, and Barbara's lovely and humorous work draws us closer to that ideal." —Craig Lesley